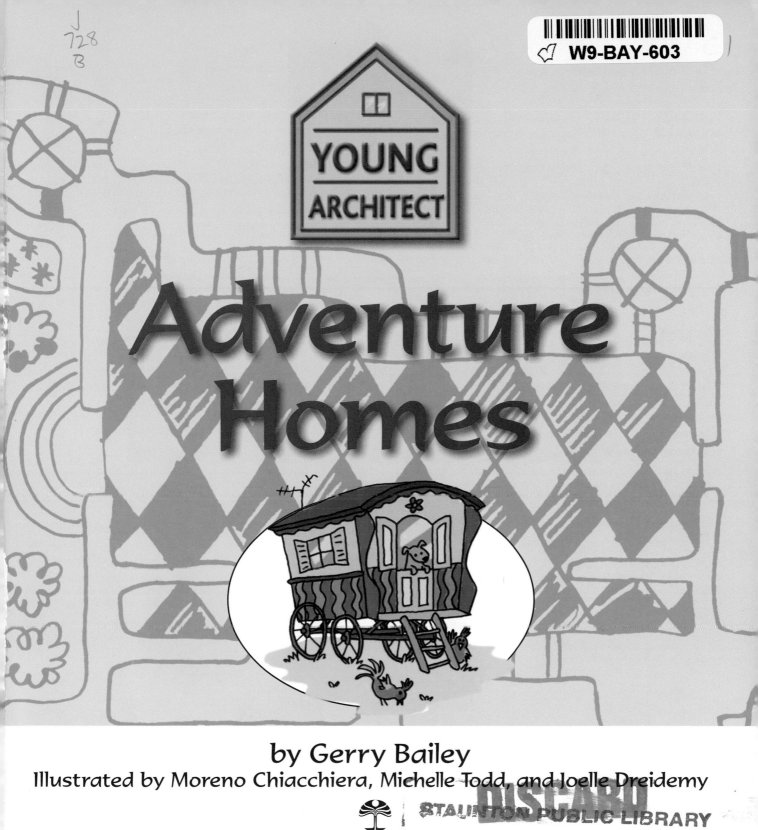

YOUNG ARCHITECT

Adventure Homes

by Gerry Bailey
Illustrated by Moreno Chiacchiera, Michelle Todd, and Joelle Dreidemy

Crabtree Publishing Company

Crabtree Publishing Company
www.crabtreebooks.com
1-800-387-7650

Published in Canada
616 Welland Ave.
St. Catharines, ON
L2M 5V6

Published in the United States
PMB 59051, 350 Fifth Ave.
59th Floor,
New York, NY

Published in 2014 by **CRABTREE PUBLISHING COMPANY**.

Author: Gerry Bailey
Illustrators: Moreno Chiacchiera, Michelle Todd,
   Joelle Dreidemy
Project coordinator: Kelly McNiven
Editor: Kathy Middleton
Proofreader: Crystal Sikkens
**Print and Production coordinator and
   Prepress technician:** Margaret Amy Salter

Photographs:
Pg 4 /5   Jeff Diener/Aurora Photos/
             Corbis
Pg 10/11   George Steinmetz/Corbis
Pg 11   George Steinmetz/Corbis
Pg 12   (tl) stable; (tr) Alexandra Glese; (b) jesadaphorn
Pg 13   Kirsz Marcin
Pg 14   Ashley Cooper/Corbis
Pg 17   ValleyStream Media 2012
Pg 18   (t) Milosz_G; (m) Draw05; (b) Gordon Wiltsie/
             National Geographic Society/Corbis
Pg 19   Potapov Igor Petrovich
Pg 20   Coprid
Pg 25   (t) Alexandra Lande; (b) Yevgen Sundikov
Pg 28   Olivier Goujon / SuperStock
Pg 29   (l) Robert Harding Picture Library / SuperStock;
             (r) Marteric

All images are Shutterstock.com unless otherwise stated.

Every attempt has been made to clear copyright. Should there be any inadvertent omission, please apply to the publisher for rectification.

Printed in Hong Kong/092013/BK20130703

Library and Archives Canada Cataloguing in Publication

Bailey, Gerry, author
      Adventure homes / by Gerry Bailey ; illustrated by Moreno Chiacchiera, Michelle Todd and Joelle Dreidemy.

 (Young architect)
Includes index.
Issued in print and electronic formats.
ISBN 978-0-7787-0287-0 (bound).--ISBN 978-0-7787-0291-7 (pbk.).--
ISBN 978-1-4271-1276-7 (pdf).--ISBN 978-1-4271-1272-9 (html)

      1. Dwellings--Juvenile literature. 2. Architecture, Domestic--Juvenile literature. I. Chiacchiera, Moreno, illustrator II. Todd, Michelle, 1978-, illustrator III. Dreidemy, Joelle, illustrator IV. Title.

GT172.B33 2013   j392.3'6   C2013-904069-2
                                                  C2013-904070-6

Library of Congress Cataloging-in-Publication Data

Bailey, Gerry.
 Adventure homes / Written by Gerry Bailey ; Illustrated by Moreno Chiacchiera, Michelle Todd, and Joelle Dreidemy.
    pages cm. -- (Young architect)
 Includes index.
 ISBN 978-0-7787-0287-0 (reinforced library binding) -- ISBN 978-0-7787-0291-7 (pbk.) --
ISBN 978-1-4271-1276-7 (electronic pdf) -- ISBN 978-1-4271-1272-9 (electronic html)
 1. Dwellings--Juvenile literature. 2. Architecture, Domestic--Juvenile literature. I. Chiacchiera, Moreno, illustrator. II. Title.

GT172.B34 2013
392.3'6--dc23

                     2013023898

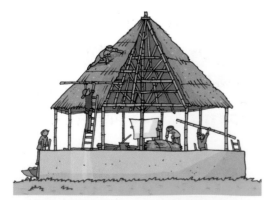

Contents

Introduction

Where do you live — in an apartment building, a townhouse, a house in the country? Sounds nice but it's a bit ordinary, isn't it? What if you lived somewhere really different, such as a house built high up in the trees, or in one that sailed from place to place whenever you wanted a change of scenery?

Or you could travel around in a **caravan**.

Well, your wish has just come true! Now you can be a young architect and design a house right out of a real adventure.

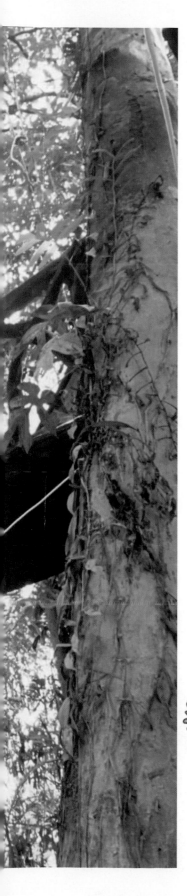

The treehouse

Wouldn't it be an adventure to build a treehouse and actually live in it? Usually a treehouse is small and built for children to play in. But some people have built full-size houses in trees so they can live in them every day.

A treehouse is usually made of wood so it will not be too heavy for the tree. Wood also blends in with the branches of the tree.

A treehouse sits on a platform high in the branches of a strong tree.

The rooms

Let's plan a tree house!

There would be an entrance by the tree's roots.

A living room would be halfway up with a balcony
where you can sit and enjoy the view.

There would be a kitchen with a table and chairs
and things to cook with.

A playroom at the top of the branches
would be big enough for all your friends.

Bedrooms would have hammocks hanging
from branches for you to sleep.

There would be nests for the birds, too.

There would be an open-air shower,
and a lookout halfway up.

Stairs would take you to the top,
but you could swing down on ropes.

A garden would grow around the bottom of the tree.

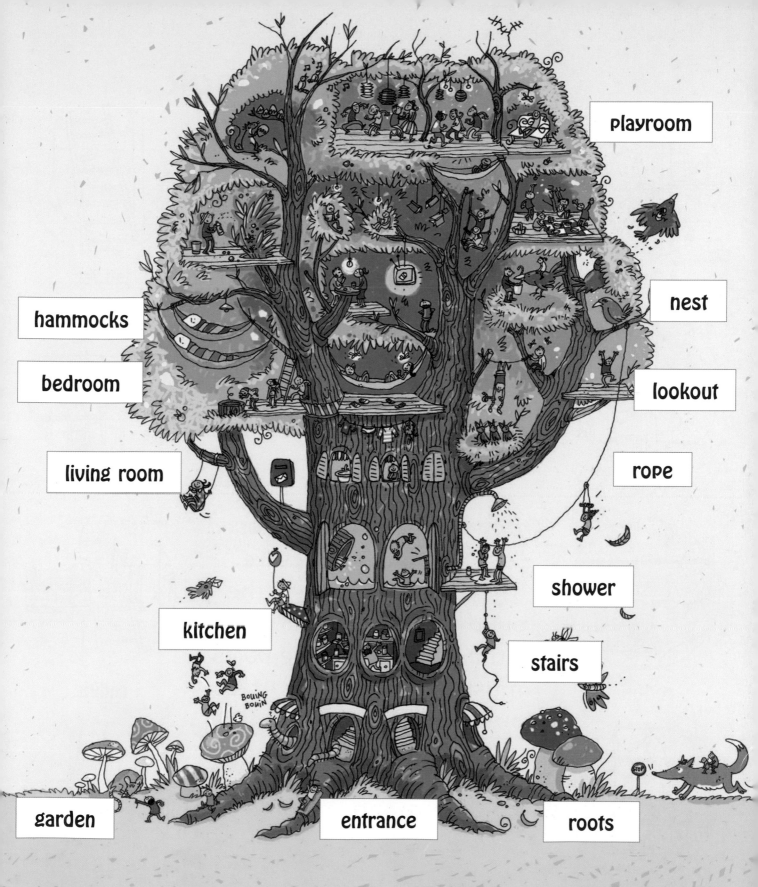

playroom

nest

hammocks

bedroom

lookout

living room

rope

shower

kitchen

stairs

garden

entrance

roots

7

Architect's notebook
- The structure -

balcony

poles

roofing

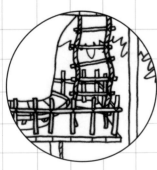

rope ladder

The overall shape and style of a building is known as its **structure**. The architect draws a detailed **plan** of the structure.

A treehouse must be built so that it is safely attached to the branches of the tree.

Often wooden poles are used as part of the structure. They are sunk deep in the ground then securely attached to the floor above. The poles must be strong enough to stop the whole structure from moving in the wind.

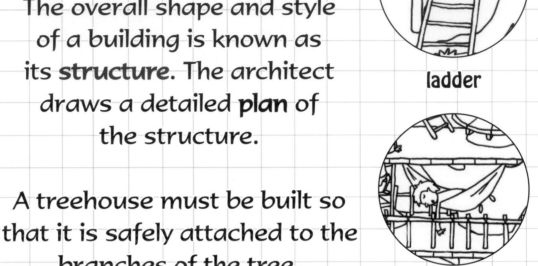

ladder

hammock

railing

swing

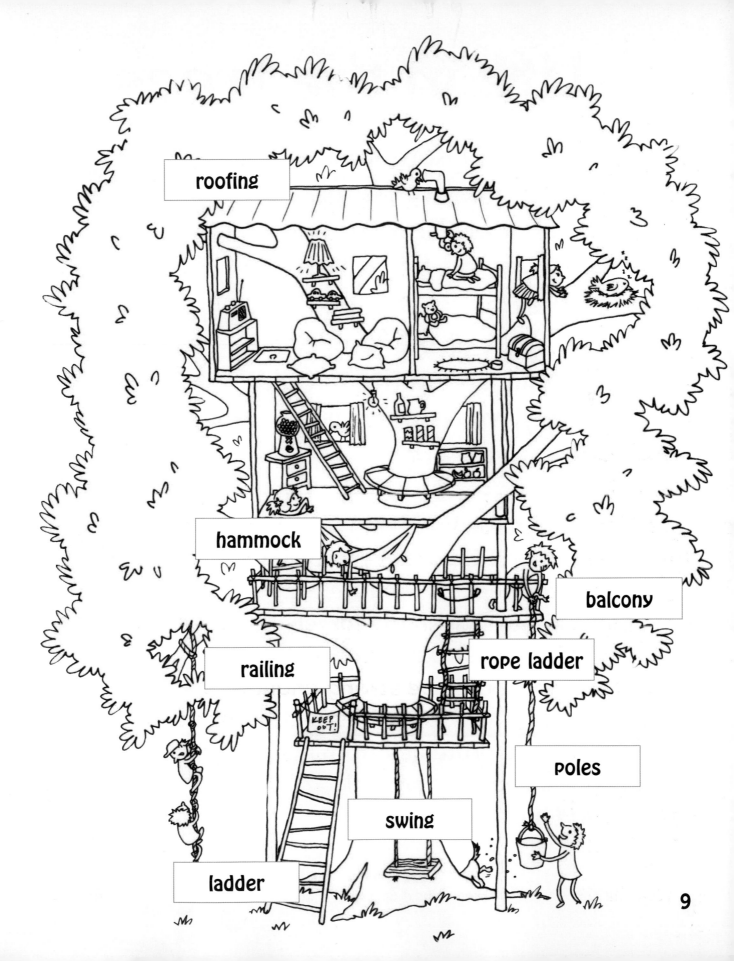

roofing

hammock

railing

ladder

balcony

rope ladder

poles

swing

KEEP OUT!

9

Life in the trees

The Korowai and Kombai are two groups of Native peoples that live in Papua New Guinea. This country is part of a large island in the Pacific Ocean, near Australia. Most of the land has not been built on, so the people and animals live as they did hundreds of years ago.

The tribes live in the huge rain forest along the Brazza River. They are often called "the tree people" because they build their homes high in the forest trees. A typical house can be as high as 130 feet (40 meters) above the ground.

Up high, they are protected from enemy tribes, flooding, and wild animals and mosquitos.

Strong wooden **stilts**, or poles, are used to hold up the treehouse.

Small tree frogs also
live in the trees.

People climb up
to the house on
a pole that has
v-shaped cuts
in it.

The building materials

Some people build their homes with **natural materials** that come from the land around them.

WOOD: Trees provide wood for the **frame**, or structure, of a house. This may come from young trees or palms.

STRAW: Straw is the dried-out stems of grass and cereal plants such as wheat, oats, rice, barley, and millet. It is often used as a roofing material called thatch.

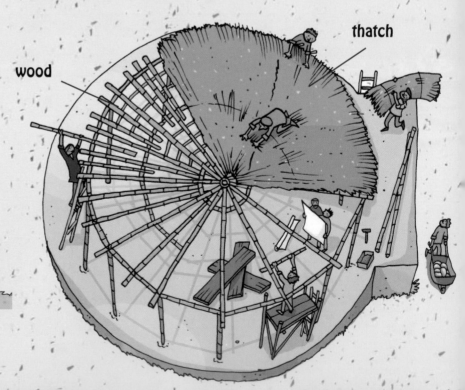

thatch

wood

MUD AND STRAW

ADOBE: **Adobe** is a building material made from a mix of sand, clay, and straw. It is packed into molds or shaped by hand into bricks. The molds are then dried in the Sun. Adobe is used to build walls or spread over the outside of a home.

The Dogon people of Mali, West Africa, grind a rock called sandstone into a muddy mix to make adobe. This soft rock is found in the hills near their home.

Home on wheels

Strong horses pull a Bow Top caravan.

How would you like to live in a home that could move from one place to another any time you like? The Romany people, called Travelers, do. Traditionally, they lived in brightly painted horse-drawn wagons called caravans. Some still do!

Travelers began living in caravans around 150 years ago. Before that they simply walked and used carts to carry their belongings. They slept in tents, called benders, that were made of twigs and covered with **canvas**.

There are several different kinds of traditional caravans.

The Reading is made of wood with a door at the front and a window at the back. The front wheels are small, and a chimney pokes out of the roof.

The Bow Top has a front door and rear windows. Its roof is made of canvas stretched over a round wooden frame.

The Burton is called the "showman's wagon." It was usually built for wealthier Travelers and was beautifully decorated. The side walls are generally straight.

Painted and carved

The inside of a Traveler's caravan is full of color. Even though it is small, it contains everything you need.

There is usually just one room inside. Some have sliding doors that hide beds for adults and children. There is a cast-iron stove for cooking, although in smaller caravans it is used only in bad weather. Cupboards and storage space are built around the main room. There is also a small table and chairs.

Birch trees make strong poles.

Spruce branches are used to cover roofs.

Home of skin

People who travel from place to place and take their homes and belongings with them are known as **nomads**. Many build tent-like homes using animal skins and wood from around the countryside.

The **lavvu** is a home used by the Sami people of northern Scandinavia. Many Sami live by raising reindeer, which provide them with food and skins for clothing and for their tents.

A lavvu is covered with reindeer skins.

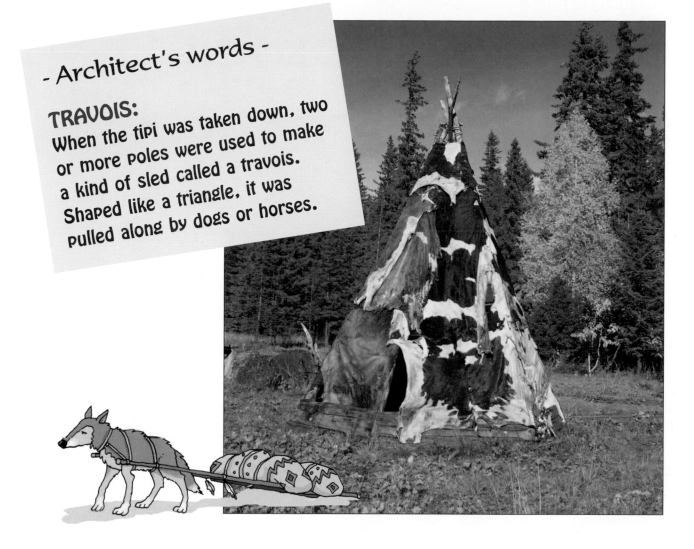

- Architect's words -

TRAVOIS:
When the tipi was taken down, two or more poles were used to make a kind of sled called a travois. Shaped like a triangle, it was pulled along by dogs or horses.

In North America, the Native peoples of the Great Plains lived in tipis. A tipi is a cone-shaped tent, with two flaps that let out the smoke from the fire inside. The fire warms the tipi and provides heat to cook with. The frame is made of poles and is covered with bison skins. Strips of skin are used to tie the poles together and wooden pegs hold the tipi to the ground. Tipis were quick and easy to take apart when it was time to move.

Tent homes

Camping is an adventure for many of us. But some people make their homes in tent-like buildings all year round. Yurts, wigwams, and tipis are kinds of portable homes used by people in the past and sometimes still today.

Nomads who live in the grassy **steppes** of Central Asia make their homes in a special tent called a yurt.

A yurt is traditionally made of a wooden frame covered by layers of material made from sheep's wool.

Architect's notebook
Build a yurt

roof poles   crown

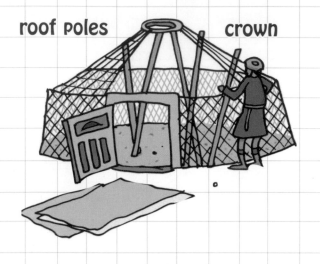

At the top of the yurt frame is a round piece called a crown.

Roof poles branch out from the crown.

The wall frame is made of latticework, or criss-crossed strips of wood. The frame is held together with rope or ribbon.

roof cover

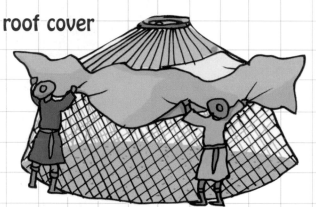

lattice frame

The yurt is covered with **felt**, a material made of sheep's wool.

Yurts are decorated with symbols of fire, water, and earth. Both real and magical animals, such as horses, lions, and dragons, are also illustrated.

A wood-burning stove is placed in the middle of the yurt. A long chimney runs from the stove and out the crown to let out smoke.

Beds and other furniture are placed around the edge of the yurt.

wall cover

Inside the yurt

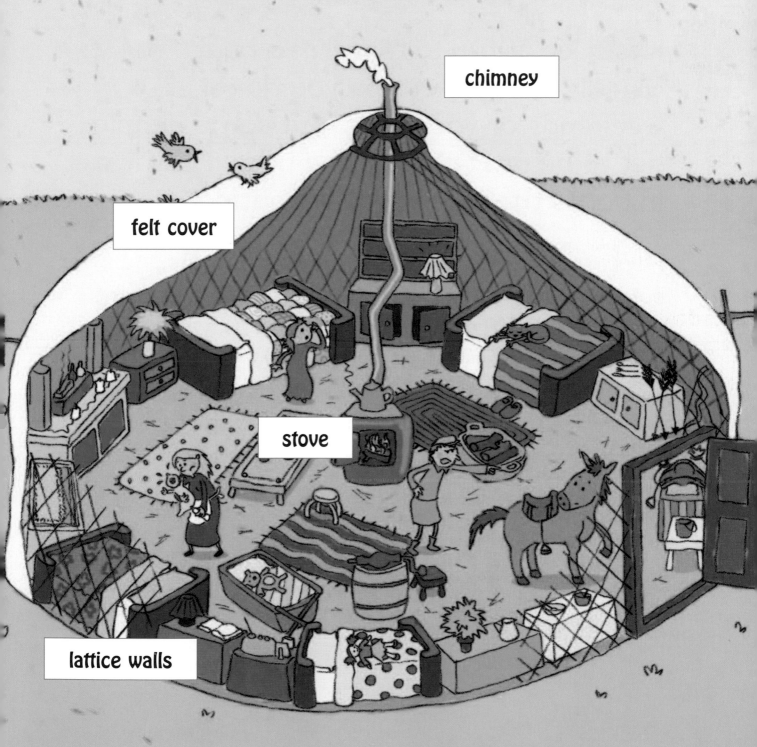

chimney

felt cover

stove

lattice walls

Floating homes

It is a lot of fun to travel in a boat. Usually it is something you do on weekends or vacations. But some people get to be on a boat all the time. They live in boats that are actually floating homes.

Floating homes include houseboats, barges, sampans, and junks. They are all built in different ways using different materials, and they are found in different parts of the world. Inside, every floating home has a kitchen, often called a galley, beds called berths to sleep in, and places to sit and enjoy life as a family.

Houseboats are made from barges that carry goods. They are often brightly decorated on the outside.

The houseboats of Kerala, India, are large, slow-moving barges about 67 feet (20 meters) long. The body is made of wooden planks, or flat boards, held together with coconut fiber ropes. The roof is made of **bamboo** poles and palm leaves.

A sampan is a wooden boat about 13 feet (4 meters) long. Used in China, sampans sail close to the seashore or on rivers.

A junk is another traditional Chinese boat. It has solid poles called **battens** that stretch across the sails, making the boat easier to control.

junk

Boat building

Long ago, most boats were made of wood because wood is light and floats easily. Today, boats may be made of different materials, such as steel and fiberglass.

bow

frame

keel

planks

stern

Boat builders begin by constructing the keel. This is the underside of the boat and is what keeps the boat from tipping over.

Then posts for the front, called the bow, and the back, called the stern, are put in place.

Next, a frame that looks like a ribcage is attached to the keel. The pieces of wood are usually steamed and bent into shape.

Planks are then placed over the frame and held in place by nails, screws, or metal pins known as rivets. The spaces between the planks have to be caulked, or sealed, to keep out water.

When the hull, or main body, of the boat is finished, the deck and living quarters are added.

Ice pillars and walls surround the visitors in this hotel.

Living in ice

Would you like an ice home? How about spending a night in an ice hotel? Inside isn't as cold as you might think!

Ice home

Ice is actually a good insulator. This means heat cannot pass through it easily. So, warm air stays inside. The Inuit people of the Arctic learned to make dome-shaped shelters called igloos out of blocks of ice and snow. Inside, they burn seal oil in lamps to make their icy homes a bit warmer.

A guest relaxes in an ice chair in the ice hotel.

An igloo is made of ice blocks.

Ice hotel

Ice hotels have more modern facilities then igloos, but they are still made of ice. Even the furniture is ice. Each year, an ice hotel is built just outside Quebec City, in Canada. It takes thousands of tons of ice to build it. It contains 85 beds with deer furs for covers. Only the bathrooms are heated in this hotel!

Glossary

adobe A building material made of sand, mud, and straw

bamboo A tall tropical grass used for building furniture

batten Strips of wood used to keep boat sails open

canvas Sturdy cloth made of hemp, flax, or cotton

felt A thick material made of wool fibers that has been pressed and rolled together

frame Support to which parts of a building are attached

insulator A material that keeps warm air inside a building

lavvu A tent covered in reindeer skin used by the Sami people of Scandinavia

natural materials Various things that are not human-made, such as wood, sand, and stone

nomad One of a wandering group of people who have no fixed home

plan An outline drawing that shows how a building will be constructed

quarters The area where someone lives

steppe A flat, treeless grassland

stilt A long pole used to raise buildings above ground or sea level

structure Another name for the framework of a building